ALBERT EINSTEIN

Albert Einstein once said, "I get most joy in life out of music.
I would have been a musician, if not a scientist."

ALBERT
EINSTEIN
A BIOGRAPHY

MILTON MELTZER

HOLIDAY HOUSE / NEW YORK

TO DAVID
AND PAUL

Library of Congress Cataloging-in-Publication Data

Meltzer, Milton, 1915–
Albert Einstein: a biography / Milton Meltzer.
p. cm.
Includes bibliographical references.
ISBN-13: 978-0-8234-1966-1 (hardcover)
1. Einstein, Albert, 1879–1955.
2. Physicists—Biography—Juvenile literature.   I. Title.
QC16.E5M45 2007
530.092—dc22
[B]
2006043676

What holds the sun and planets in space? Does space go on forever? What makes the sky blue? Where does math come from, and who thought it up?

Albert Einstein was always asking questions. He worked hard all his life to find the answers. By the time he was twenty-six, his original thinking had transformed our understanding of the natural world. His scientific theories had practical effects too. They prepared the way for great new things—from space exploration and computers to lasers and nuclear power.

As brilliant as Einstein was, he was very human. Like you and me, he knew joy and misery, success and failure. "Anyone who has never made a mistake," he once said, "has never tried anything new." He challenged not only what scientists took as proven, but also the way nations are governed, and the way too many people are forced to live—and die.

He asked questions constantly, seeking to learn why things are the way they are, and believing we can change them for the better. Long before Einstein died, the world acclaimed him as being among the greatest scientists of all time.

Sometimes out of the smallest places come the greatest people. On March 14, 1879, Albert Einstein was born in the small town of Ulm, Germany. He was the first child of Hermann and Pauline Einstein.

His father and uncle Jakob ran a small electrical supply company. Hoping to do more business, they moved to the big city of Munich, where Albert's sister, Maja, was born.

After centuries of discrimination, in 1848 Germany had granted Jews full citizenship. The Einsteins thought anti-Semitism would shortly disappear. And Albert's generation would enjoy the chance to rise, so long denied to Jews.

Papa and Mama had high hopes for their son. Before he was even three, he tried to speak in whole sentences. First he practiced the words softly to himself, then said

Albert and his younger sister, Maja

them aloud. He loved the music his mother played on the piano. At five he began playing the violin, giving it a pet name, Lina. Later he would say, "I get most joy in life out of music. I would have been a musician, if not a scientist."

Albert began school when he was six. He was the only Jew in the class. It made him feel like an outsider. The school was run army-style, with the strictest discipline. You accepted what the teachers told you, and that was that. Albert didn't like it. The teachers called him a dreamer. Still, he earned high marks.

At about age eleven Albert entered high school. But again, it was mostly "babbling from memory," he said. Names! Dates! Facts! Ask no questions! No time for ideas.

Luckily he found pleasure in learning outside the classroom.

One day Uncle Jakob handed Albert a geometry book. Albert tried to prove one theorem his own way—and did it. Mathematics is a merry science, his uncle said. "When the animal that we are hunting cannot be caught, we call it X temporarily and continue to hunt it until it is bagged."

In these years a young medical student often visited the family. He brought Albert books on science, and they spent hours discussing ideas. Albert and his mama would often play Mozart, Schubert, or Beethoven pieces during the evenings, Albert on his violin and his mother on the piano.

As Albert's first year in high school ended, his father's business fell off badly. The family moved to Milan, hoping sales would improve in Italy. Albert was left behind to live with a relative till graduation. But after a few months he felt he couldn't stand three more years of this miserable school. He quit and rejoined his family.

This didn't please his parents. Who did he think he was?

Albert knew who he was, even if they didn't. To add to his family's alarm, Albert gave up his German citizenship. He hated the military regime that now dominated life in Germany. And he would not accept being forced into military service. He meant to be master of his own destiny, not the tool of a war-minded government.

Albert tried to enter the highly regarded Polytechnic Institute in Zurich, Switzerland. Although you had to be eighteen to enroll and he was only sixteen, Albert was allowed to take the entrance exams. He scored high in math and science, but low in history and languages. To fill in these gaps, he went to another school in a nearby town.

One day, he later recalled, he was watching sunlight reflecting off the surface of a lake when an odd image came to him. "What would it be like to ride a beam of sunlight? At sixteen I had no idea, but the question stayed with me for the next ten years. The simplest questions are always the hardest. But if I have one gift, it is that I am as stubborn as a mule." Trying to understand the nature of light set Albert on a path that would lead to his most famous work—the theory of relativity.

At the end of the year Albert graduated with an outstanding record and passed all his entrance exams for the Polytechnic. He had decided to make theoretical physics—a branch of science that deals with matter and energy and their relationship to each other—his field.

At Polytechnic Albert didn't behave like most students. He went only to those classes that interested him. He preferred to study the ideas of the best scientists on his own. But he did work on laboratory experiments in physics.

The few friends Albert made at school were close ones. And girls liked this good-looking teenager, with his great mop of black hair and stylish mustache. He

By 1920 Albert Einstein had already written his remarkable papers on relativity that made him famous. He was awarded the Nobel Prize in Physics in 1921.

was fun to be with, banging away at the piano or sawing on his fiddle, and there seemed to be no end to his amusing chatter.

In 1900 Albert received his degree from Polytechnic Institute. For two years he hunted for work in his field. But all he could find were part-time positions teaching in village schools.

Meanwhile, he worked up his original ideas into his first scientific paper; and although he was now only twenty-two and a "nobody" in the world of physics, a German physics journal published his paper.

Then in 1902 came a change of luck. Albert was appointed a technical expert at the Swiss Federal Patent Office in Bern. His job was to study inventions, especially electrical devices, and see if they were worthy of patents. You'd think the work was unworthy of a genius, but Albert didn't see it that way. As a college professor he would have been spending untold hours and energy preparing for classes and worrying about promotions. But this job left him plenty of time to think about problems in physics. Here, he said later, "is where I hatched my most beautiful ideas."

His salary was enough to support a family, and early in 1903 Albert married Mileva Maric, a classmate at the Polytechnic. Four years older than Albert, she was a Serb, and the only woman in his class. Because Albert's family strongly opposed her, it had been a long time before they married.

Those years in the patent office were Einstein's most creative time. Sitting at his desk, at home in their apartment, or while out walking, he kept asking questions, seeking to understand the makeup of the universe. He reviewed long-held theories of many other scientists, even the greatest, such as Isaac Newton. He refused to take anything on faith. And in 1905 a German scientific journal, the *Annals of Physics*, published a series of three Einstein papers that would create a revolution in physics.

In the first paper Einstein demonstrated that light is not only a wave, but also a particle. And it is the fastest thing in the universe. It travels at the speed of 186 thousand miles per second, or 670 million miles per hour. It takes a commercial jet plane about six hours to fly from New York to California. But light can go there and back in one-thirtieth of a second! Why nothing travels faster than light is a mystery scientists have yet to solve.

In the second paper Einstein proved that molecules exist and that their sizes can be calculated. The third paper—on "special relativity"—completely changed the general view of space and time.

Before Einstein, it was believed that space and time were absolute—that is, they never changed. Einstein said that they are elastic, or relative, and that mass and energy are two forms of the same thing. He looked for the source of energy in the one place no one else had ever looked—in solid matter itself. He gave a formula for that equivalence: $E = mc^2$.

E stands for energy. It's what makes things happen—moving your shopping cart or heating your soup. Energy can change from one form to another. It exists in many forms, such as heat and light.

M stands for mass. Mass is the amount of "stuff" all physical objects have. It's not connected to size. A box of tissues, for instance, can be the same size as a brick, but they have different masses. (Imagine the difference between dropping the tissue box on your foot and then the brick.)

Einstein's figures on the speed of light, $E = mc^2$

No matter what you do to these physical objects—drop them, hammer them, squeeze them—they won't disappear. They just combine or recombine. And the total mass of all the substances that fill the universe remains the same.

The c in the formula refers to the speed of light: 186 thousand miles per second, or 670 million miles per hour. Einstein's theory states that this is a constant and that nothing can ever travel faster. In his equation, c is squared, which means you multiply 670 million miles per hour by 670 million miles per hour.

Until Einstein, no one thought that anything connected energy and mass. But with a flash of insight he saw that neither energy nor mass stands alone. They could be connected, and the speed of light was the bridge. A very small amount of mass can become tremendously magnified whenever it passes through that equation and comes out on the side of energy. As an example, if you converted the tiny mass in a paper clip into energy, it could light millions of homes for a year.

Einstein worked out his great ideas in an incredibly short time. During a period of eight months in 1905, while putting in a full six-day week at the patent office, he came up with his equation $E = mc^2$. What he figured out helped prepare the way for lasers, computer chips, advances in the bioengineering and pharmaceutical industries, and all Internet switching devices.

Ten years after developing his formula, Einstein published his general theory of relativity, going beyond the remarkable achievement of the earlier work.

Einstein's equation was a theory that scientists came to accept as true. Yes, matter could be transformed so that energy within it could be let out. But how could you really make that happen?

Albert Einstein with another scientist whose work changed the world, Marie Curie

Most physicists are either theorizers or experimenters. A theory holds that something should work. An experiment proves that it does—or doesn't. Einstein theorized how things worked, but it took quite a while before experimental technology had developed enough to prove that his theory really did work.

For many years scientists in various parts of the world studied the relativity theory and performed experiments to test their ideas. Not until the 1930s were physicists able to show how the compressed energy that $E = mc^2$ spoke about could be let out. They came up with a method for cracking apart the nucleus, the central core of each atom that makes up matter, which releases enormous bursts of energy. The discovery of nuclear fission made possible the development of nuclear weapons.

Historians of science see Einstein's work as the seed that flowered in many other fields: astrophysics, cosmology, nuclear physics, electronics, space travel. The vision and imagination of a twenty-six-year-old changed science and society beyond measure.

During Einstein's seven years at the patent office, his two sons, Hans Albert and Eduard, were born. And Ein-

Three generations of Einsteins: Albert, his son Hans Albert (left), and his grandson, Bernhard (center)

stein's fame led to a series of professorships. The best came in 1914: professor at the University of Berlin, together with a research post and leadership of a new institute for physics.

Unhappily, Albert and Mileva separated soon after. Mileva and the two boys returned to Zurich, and Albert became a bachelor again.

In 1914 World War I broke out. Germany, Austria-Hungary, and Turkey were on one side, and most of the other European nations, plus the United States and Japan, were on the other. Einstein had always been against war. When many German scientists proclaimed that Germany's cause was just, he was furious. He publicly denounced them. War is insane, he said, and destructive of life, of human progress, of science.

Few listened to him, for he was not yet a world-famous figure. He continued his studies through the war years. In 1919, soon after his divorce from Mileva, he married his cousin Elsa. Just then great news flashed around the world. Two British scientists making astronomical observations of a solar eclipse had confirmed Einstein's general theory of relativity! That theory had predicted exactly to what extent a light beam would be bent when it passes near the sun. It also predicted that the universe must be expanding.

In 1921 Albert was awarded the Nobel Prize in

Einstein was well-known for his wit. "Do not worry about your problems with mathematics, I assure you mine are far greater."

Physics (although for a lesser discovery, not his general theory of relativity). He gave the prize money to Mileva to support her and their sons. Albert became a world celebrity overnight.

Did such recognition make him arrogant? "All I have tried is to ask a few questions," he said. He believed that in their search for knowledge and truth, scientists must be free to think, investigate, and act independently. No one, whether government or society, has the right to interfere with the scientist's freedom of inquiry.

Once, laughing at still another request for a simple explanation of relativity, Einstein said, "When a man sits with a pretty girl for an hour, it seems to him a minute. But let him sit on a hot stove for only a minute—and it's longer than an hour. That's relativity."

From early on it was clear that Einstein was interested not only in science. Now more than ever he felt it his duty to use his worldwide fame to advance movements for peace, for international unity, and for social justice.

When Adolf Hitler came to power in Germany in January 1933, everything decent people cherished—peace, freedom, democracy—was smashed. Hitler set up a brutal dictatorship, and Jews especially were in grave danger. "I did not wish to live in a country," Einstein said, "where the individual does not enjoy equality before the law and freedom to say and teach what he likes." In September 1933 Einstein accepted the invitation of Princeton University to join its newly established Institute for Advanced Study.

With no obligation to teach, he followed his own path. For the rest of his life he hoped to develop a "complete theory" that would explain all the forces and phenomena in the whole universe. But he did not succeed. Scientists are still trying to figure out a "theory of everything."

Word reached Einstein in 1939 that Hitler's scientists might make an atomic bomb. He wrote President Franklin D. Roosevelt, urging that America move quickly before the Nazis could attack with this horribly destructive weapon. The president promptly created the secret Manhattan Project to develop an atomic bomb.

It was a hard moral decision for Einstein. He had always opposed wars of any kind. But he realized that nonviolent resistance to Hitler's power was no longer enough.

Einstein never joined the atomic bomb project. When America dropped atomic bombs on the Japanese cities of

Hiroshima and Nagasaki in 1945, he was horrified. When World War II ended in 1945, the terrible news of the Holocaust became known. Hitler had killed many millions of innocent men, women, and children, six million of them Jews. The fact that Einstein's homeland had done this was almost too much for him to bear.

Einstein renewed his pursuit of peace for all nations and campaigned for nuclear disarmament, for civil liberties and civil rights, and for an end to racism and poverty. He spoke up boldly, even when it meant taking unpopular, even dangerous, positions.

And his personal losses began to mount. His parents had died long ago, then his sister, Maja, and his wives, Mileva and Elsa. He himself, reaching seventy, was sick with heart trouble.

In April 1955 he collapsed at his home in Princeton, and on the eighteenth he died. He was seventy-six.

A great man was gone, but not what he loved, what he stood for, what he fought for—the constant struggle

Einstein's 1939 letter to President Franklin D. Roosevelt warned him of the possibility of atomic bombs. Later, he regretted writing the letter, which led to the invention and use of atomic bombs.

Albert Einstein
Old Grove Rd.
Nassau Point
Peconic, Long Island

August 2nd, 1939

F.D. Roosevelt,
President of the United States,
White House
Washington, D.C.

Sir:

Some recent work by E.Fermi and L. Szilard, which has been com-
municated to me in manuscript, leads me to expect that the element uranium may be turned into a new and important source of energy in the immediate future. Certain aspects of the situation which has arisen seem
to call for watchfulness and, if necessary, quick action on the part
of the Administration. I believe therefore that it is my duty to bring
to your attention the following facts and recommendations:

In the course of the last four months it has been made probable -
through the work of Joliot in France as well as Fermi and Szilard in
America - that it may become possible to set up a nuclear chain reaction
in a large mass of uranium,by which vast amounts of power and large quant-
ities of new radium-like elements would be generated. Now it appears
almost certain that this could be achieved in the immediate future.

This new phenomenon would also lead to the construction of bombs,
and it is conceivable - though much less certain - that extremely power-
ful bombs of a new type may thus be constructed. A single bomb of this
type, carried by boat and exploded in a port, might very well destroy
the whole port together with some of the surrounding territory. However,
such bombs might very well prove to be too heavy for transportation by
air.

Einstein's study in Princeton, New Jersey, where he continued
his scientific work after moving to the United States
in 1933 to escape the Nazis

to understand the nature of the universe, faith in human progress, the search for lasting peace. He once said, "There is no higher religion than human service. To work for the common good is the greatest creed."

Albert Einstein celebrating his seventieth birthday

BIBLIOGRAPHY

Balibar, Françoise. *Einstein: Decoding the Universe* (Discoveries). New York: Harry N. Abrams, 2001.

Bodanis, David. *$E = mc^2$: A Biography of the World's Most Famous Equation.* New York: Berkley Publishing Group, 2000.

Calaprice, Alice, ed. *Dear Professor Einstein: Albert Einstein's Letters to and from Children.* Amherst, NY: Prometheus Books, 2002.

Einstein, Albert. *Ideas and Opinions.* New York: Dell Publishing, 1973.

Jerome, Fred. *The Einstein File: J. Edgar Hoover's Secret War Against the World's Most Famous Scientist.* New York: St. Martin's Press, 2002.

Overbye, Dennis. *Einstein in Love: A Scientific Romance.* New York: Viking Penguin, 2000.

Pais, Abraham. *Subtle Is the Lord: The Science and the Life of Albert Einstein.* New York: Oxford University Press, 1982.

Parker, Barry. *Einstein's Brainchild: Relativity Made Relatively Easy!* Amherst, NY: Prometheus Books, 2000.

Schwartz, Joseph, and Michael McGuinness. *Einstein for Beginners.* New York: Pantheon Books, 1979.

Stern, Fritz. *Einstein's German World.* Princeton, NJ: Princeton University Press, 1999.

White, Michael, and John Gribbin. *Einstein: A Life in Science.* New York: Dutton, 1994.

Einstein walking in his garden

TIME LINE

1879	Born March 14 in Ulm, Germany.
1885–1896	Schooling.
1895	Renounces his German citizenship.
1896–1900	Studies at Polytechnic Institute (later the Federal Institute of Technology) in Zurich, Switzerland.
1901	Acquires Swiss citizenship. Completes his first scientific paper.
1902	Appointed technical expert at the Swiss Federal Patent Office in Bern.
1905	Publishes three papers that completely revolutionize the concepts of time and space, energy and matter. Initial version of $E = mc^2$ appears in print for the first time. Receives PhD from Zurich University.
1909	Resigns from patent office.
1911	Predicts bending of light by gravity.
1911–1917	Works as professor of theoretical physics at Prague, Zurich, and Berlin.
1916	His general theory of relativity is published.
1919	His theories on light and gravity are confirmed by eclipse observations. Becomes a world figure.

1921	Awarded Nobel Prize in Physics. First visit to the United States.
1922	Completes first paper on unified field theory.
1925	Signs manifesto against compulsory military service.
1930	Becomes intensely active on behalf of pacifism.
1932–1933	Leaves Germany for the United States. Appointed professor at the Institute for Advanced Study at Princeton University.
1939	Signs letter to President Franklin D. Roosevelt recommending U.S. research on nuclear weapons.
1940	Becomes U.S. citizen.
1943	Works as research consultant for the U.S. Navy during World War II.
1946–1947	Becomes chairman of the Emergency Committee of Atomic Scientists. Voices support for disarmament and formation of a world government.
1948	Supports creation of the State of Israel.
1952	Offered presidency of the State of Israel but declines.
1953	Publicly supports individuals investigated by House Un-American Activities Committee.
1955	Cosigns the Russell-Einstein Manifesto, warning of nuclear war and appealing for nuclear disarmament.
	Dies April 18 in Princeton Hospital at the age of seventy-six.

PHOTO CREDITS